Claire East and Hannah Bull are the best of friends.

They even have their own handshake.

Then one day, Hannah said she did not want to be Claire's friend anymore.

Claire is sad that Hannah doesn't want to be her friend. She sits on a swing alone.

Then Hannah and Danica walk by and use the *same* handshake that Claire and Hannah used to have.

Claire asks if she could play with Hannah and Danica.

But they leave her out.

Claire held in the tears while Hannah and Danica were there, but once they leave, Claire begins to cry.

How do you think this story might end?
Write or draw your ideas.

Four Possible Endings

Ending #1:
New Friend

A new girl named Sheryl Newfrind sees
Claire crying

Sheryl comes up and asks Claire why she is sad.

Why are you crying?

Claire answers, "Those girls won't play with me. Hannah said she doesn't want to be my friend anymore."

Sheryl says, "It sounds like they were bullying you; you did nothing wrong."

Claire listens as Sheryl explains bullying.

Sheryl says, "Sometimes people bully by hitting. Other times they call names and other times they bully by saying they won't be your friend anymore, even if you did nothing wrong."

Claire feels much better after talking to Sheryl.

Claire isn't bothered by Hannah or Danica anymore.

Friendship always wins!

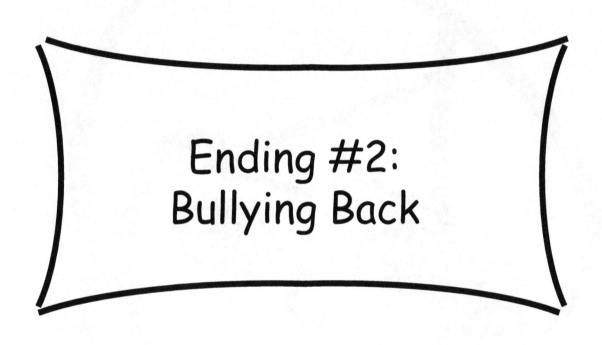

Ending #2:
Bullying Back

After a little while, Claire feels like talking to Hannah and Danica.

Claire walks over to Hannah and Danica with confidence and asks why they used her handshake.

Hannah says, "I don't see why it's such a big deal."

24

Claire replies, "But it was *our* handshake! And it hurts my feelings to see you using it without me."

Hannah rolls her eyes and says, "This is why I don't want to be your friend; you're such a baby!"

Claire, holding back tears, can't stand it anymore and kicks sand at Hannah.

Hannah runs away, pretending to cry as she finds a teacher so she can tell on Claire.

Claire has to sit out the rest of recess that day, and thinks about Hannah and Danica. She wishes she hadn't let them bother her.

29

The next day while Claire is swinging, she sees Hannah and Danica using the handshake.

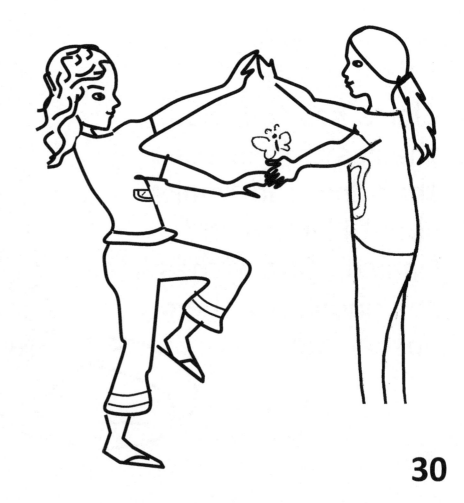

This ending is not happy; bullying back is never a good idea.

Ending #3:
Making Up

The next day, after Claire feels better, she confronts Danica.

Claire asks, "Why did you steal Hannah from me?"

Danica looks a little hurt and says, "I didn't know I was stealing Hannah from you!"

Claire replies, "But that handshake you use with Hannah used to be our handshake."

36

Danica says, "Really? Hannah said she made it up. I didn't know it used to be yours."

Claire is happy to hear Danica wasn't purposely being mean to her. Claire explains her side of the story, "It really hurt my feelings."

Danica says, "I'm sorry. I didn't know it was hurting you."

Danica suggests, "Maybe we should talk to Hannah; there's no reason why we shouldn't all be friends."

Danica and Claire approach Hannah.

Hannah seems hesitant to be Claire's friend, but she agrees.

After a while, Hannah is friendlier to Claire and they are all better friends.

Ending #4:
Getting Adult Help

After school that day, Claire decides to talk to someone about the situation.

Counselor

Claire explains everything to the counselor.

The counselor explains, "Sometimes kids who don't feel important in other ways use a bad kind of power. The kind of power that hurts people. Sometimes bullies hurt by hitting. Sometimes bullies hurt by saying words that make people feel bad. It isn't your fault."

Claire looks up and says, "It isn't?"

The counselor responds, "No, bullies usually only bully because they want to feel better about themselves. Sometimes they don't know how to be a good friend."

The counselor says, "What would you like to happen next? Do you have any ideas?"

Claire replies, "I just want them to be nice to me and not leave me out of their games."

The counselor says, "I have two ideas. First, I can supervise the playground this week, and I can talk to Hannah and Danica if I see them being mean to anyone. Second, we can have a workshop on how to be a good friend."

Claire agrees with the two ideas and leaves the counselor's office feeling much better.

Counselor

The next week, a Girl Scout troop came to Claire's school and taught bully prevention.

P☮wer Up↑

Doing nothing? Not an option.

Keys to Helping:
- Doing Nothing? Not an Option!
- Everyone stays safe, and keeps her dignity.
- Don't bully back

After that workshop, Claire wasn't bothered by Hannah or Danica anymore. She made new friends instead.

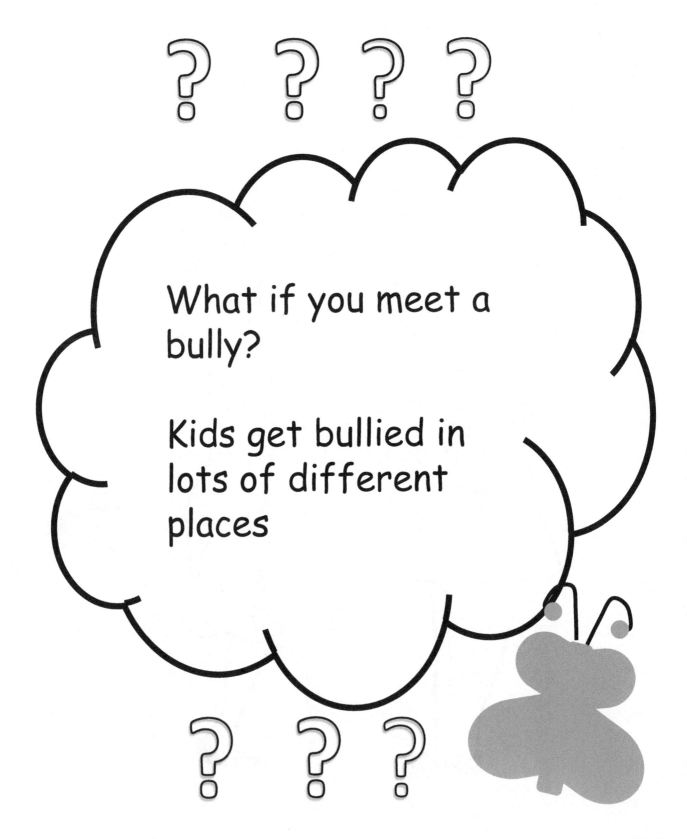

What if you meet a bully?

Kids get bullied in lots of different places

Some get bullied on the bus

Some get bullied on the playground

Some get bullied at school

Some get bullied on the computer

Some get bullied in Girl Scouts or in another after-school club or activity.

Read the following scenes and act out your ideas. Use the paper dolls to show what you might do. It might be fun to do this activity with a friend or talk about your ideas with a trusted adult.

You are playing a game with your friend. You are really good at this game and almost always win. Your friend says, "You're a cheater. I'm not going to play with you anymore." You know you didn't cheat. What can you do or say?

Every girl in your class, except you, got invited to a party. You really want to go. How do you feel? What can you say or do?

Your older brother blames you when something goes wrong. Today, he told your dad you broke the DVD player. Actually, your brother broke it, but no one else was around to see what happened. What can you do or say?

A big, older girl at your school threatens to beat you up if you don't give her part of your allowance every week. What can you do or say?

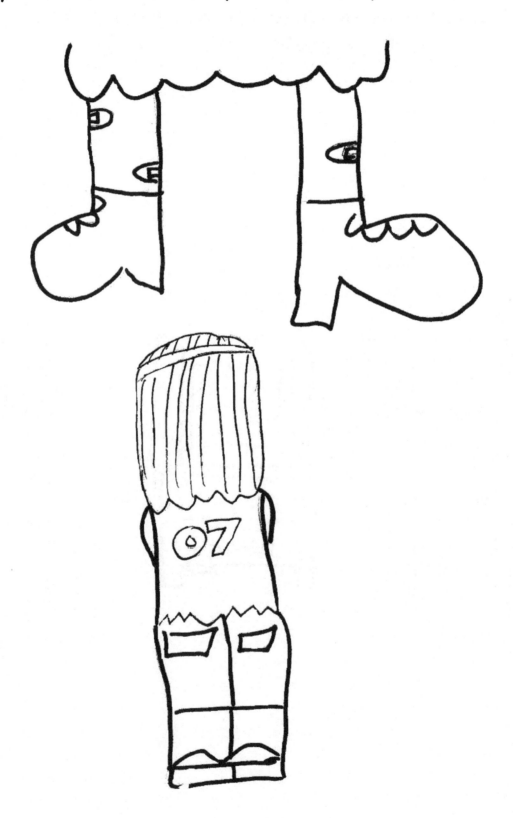

Whenever the teacher is out of the room, one of the boys tickles your best friend. She tells him to stop, but he doesn't listen. What can you do or say?

A couple of girls in your class talk in really low voices to a girl who wears a hearing aid. When she asks them to repeat what they said, they run away giggling. What can you say or do?

Your mom tells you she saw one of your friends kick her dog. What can you say or do?

A girl you hardly know in school e-mails a horrible photo of you to a bunch of kids. The caption on top of the photo reads: "Don't be friends with this LOSER" Your best friend shows you the photo and message. What can you say or do?

Ever been a bully?

If you sometimes act like a bully, here are some tips.

Think about how kids feel when you tease or hurt them. Put yourself in their place.

Talk to a trusted adult or older brother, sister, or cousin about how you feel when you act like a bully.

Decide one thing you're going to do right now to stop being a bully.

Take one action to become the kind of person you're proud to be. What did you do?

_____

Are you kind and strong? Even when people are powerful and strong, they can be kind to each other.

Tell a story of good power and kindness using paper dolls in a puppet show.

Use your Power to Make the World a better place

75

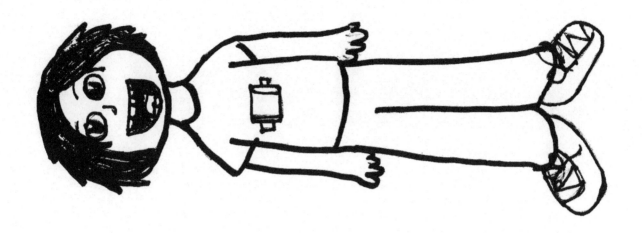

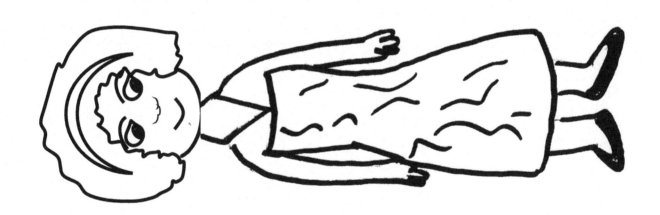

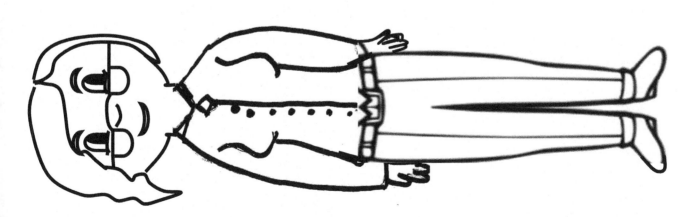

79

Made in the USA
Las Vegas, NV
18 February 2022

44144518R00044